Or have each member of your band pick one word sile

NOUN	NOUN	NOU	
BOOKS	TRAINS	AFICIONADOS	AHOY
TREES	BASES	BUCCANEERS	BADA-BING
CARS	INSTITUTES	JAMBALAYA	YA-YAH
JACKETS	WIZARDS	ENIGMAS	WHAT
DOORS	EYEBALLS	CRUXES	YUM
WALLABIES	PUGS	CZARS	JUNIOR
DREAMS	MYTHS	HOOLIGANS	LA-DI-DAH
LOVE	SPELLS	JALOPIES	AYE
FEET	SWITCHES	CLAPTRAP	DUH
LIPS	ALIENS	PARTNERS	TA-DA
PAPER CLIPS	ROCKETS	SERENDIPITY	YUCK
ROSES	BAZOOKAS	TINTINNABULATION	ZOWIE
UNICORNS	TEDDIES	MOXIE	HEY
THUNDER	EARTHQUAKES	RUMPUS	OOH-LA-LA
PRINCESSES	TRUTH	[PICK A FRUIT!]	NOW

ISBN 978-1-4521-4535-8

Manufactured in China.

Design by Nadia Izazi and Ryan Hayes.
Typeset in Brandon Grotesque.
The illustrations in this book were
rendered digitally.

10 9 8 7 6 5 4 3 2 1

Chronicle Books LLC
680 Second Street
San Francisco, CA 94107

Location: ________________ Date: ________________

SONG TITLE:

Artist

Album:

Label:

Duration:

Genre:

Source:

Who I want to share this song with:

How I discovered this song:

Playlists to put this song on:

RATING:

Lyrics

Sound quality

Catchiness

Vocals

Mood it puts me in

Instrumentation

INSTRUMENTS IN THE SONG:

☐ Other:

FAVORITE LYRIC:

THOUGHTS:

MOOD BOARD:

Location: ______________ Date: ______________

SONG TITLE: ______________

Artist ______________

Album: ______________

Label: ______________

Duration: ______________

Genre: ______________

Source: ______________

Who I want to share this song with: ______________

How I discovered this song: ______________

Playlists to put this song on: ______________

RATING:

INSTRUMENTS IN THE SONG:

☐ ☐ ☐

☐ ☐ ☐

☐ ☐ ☐

☐ ☐ ☐

☐ Other: ______________

FAVORITE LYRIC:

THOUGHTS:

MOOD BOARD:

Location: ______ Date: ______

SONG TITLE:

Artist

Album:

Label:

Duration:

Genre:

Source:

Who I want to share this song with:

How I discovered this song:

Playlists to put this song on:

RATING:

Lyrics
Sound quality
Catchiness
Vocals
Mood it puts me in
Instrumentation

INSTRUMENTS IN THE SONG:

☐ Other:

FAVORITE LYRIC:

THOUGHTS:

MOOD BOARD:

A. PLAYLIST FOR

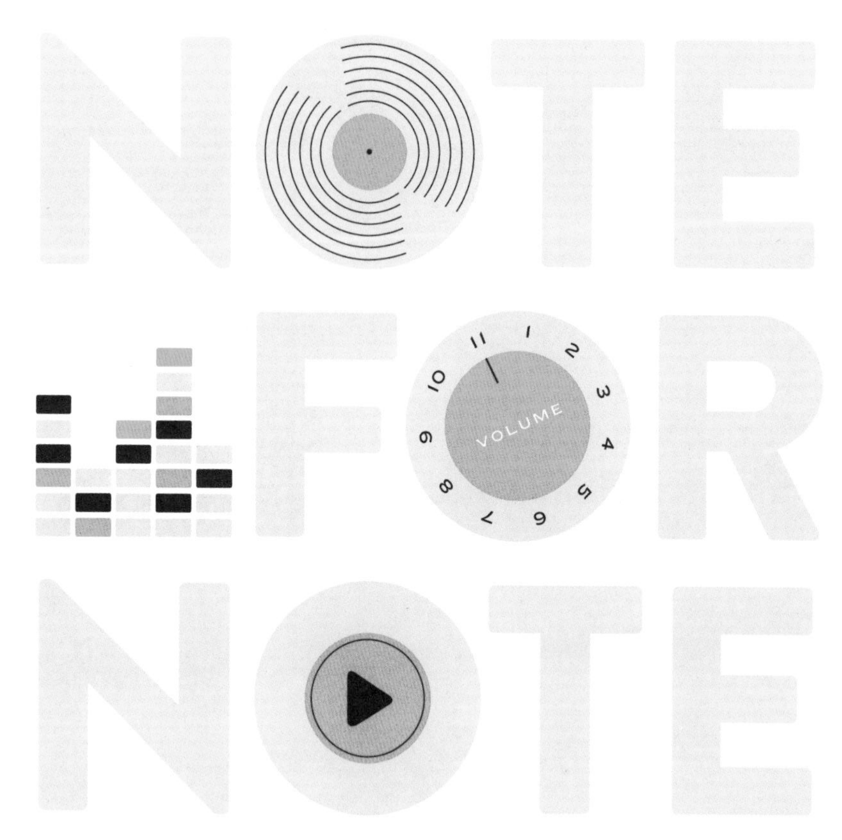

A MUSIC JOURNAL

CHRONICLE BOOKS
SAN FRANCISCO

Location: Bedroom Date: Oct. 25TH

SONG TITLE: Ring of Fire

Artist: Johnny Cash

Album: Ring of Fire: The Best of Johnny Cash

Label: Colombia

Duration: 2:38

Genre: Rock and Roll

Source: CD

Who I want to share this song with: Alexa

How I discovered this song: Heard on the radio

Playlists to put this song on: "Gritty Rock"

RATING:

Lyrics
Sound quality
Vocals
Instrumentation
Mood it puts me in
Catchiness

INSTRUMENTS IN THE SONG:

- [x] Acoustic guitar
- [ ] Flying V guitar
- [x] Electric guitar
- [x] Drum kit
- [ ] Microphone
- [ ] Keyboard
- [ ] Piano
- [ ] Saxophone
- [x] Trumpet
- [ ] Trombone
- [ ] Drum
- [ ] Violin
- [ ] Other:

FAVORITE LYRIC:

I fell for you like a child. Oh, but the fire went wild.

THOUGHTS:

- It seems like the song would be negative about love based on the title, but the lyrics are mostly about the passion of falling in love.

- That said, I could see people thinking the song is maybe about how love, while it's an extremely strong feeling, can really hurt.

MOOD BOARD:

Location: ______ Date: ______

SONG TITLE: ______

Artist ______

Album: ______

Label: ______

Duration: ______

Genre: ______

Source: ______

Who I want to share this song with: ______

How I discovered this song: ______

Playlists to put this song on: ______

RATING:

Lyrics
Sound quality
Catchiness
Vocals
Mood it puts me in
Instrumentation

INSTRUMENTS IN THE SONG:

☐ ☐ ☐
☐ ☐ ☐
☐ ☐ ☐
☐ ☐ ☐

☐ Other: ______

FAVORITE LYRIC:

THOUGHTS:

MOOD BOARD:

Location: ______________________ Date: ____________

SONG TITLE: ______________________

Artist ______________________

Album: ______________________

Label: ______________________

Duration: ______________________

Genre: ______________________

Source: ______________________

Who I want to share this song with: ______________

How I discovered this song: ______________

Playlists to put this song on: ______________

____

RATING:

Lyrics

Sound quality

Vocals

Instrumentation

Mood it puts me in

Catchiness

INSTRUMENTS IN THE SONG:

☐ ☐ ☐

☐ ☐ ☐

☐ ☐ ☐

☐ ☐ ☐

☐ Other: ______________________

____

FAVORITE LYRIC:

____

THOUGHTS:

MOOD BOARD:

Location: ______ Date: ______

SONG TITLE: ______

Artist ______

Album: ______

Label: ______

Duration: ______

Genre: ______

Source: ______

Who I want to share this song with: ______

How I discovered this song: ______

Playlists to put this song on: ______

RATING:

Lyrics
Sound quality
Catchiness
Vocals
Mood it puts me in
Instrumentation

INSTRUMENTS IN THE SONG:

☐ ☐ ☐

☐ ☐ ☐

☐ ☐ ☐

☐ ☐ ☐

☐ Other: ______

FAVORITE LYRIC:

THOUGHTS:

MOOD BOARD:

IF I WERE...

A ROCK STAR

HOW WOULD I BE?

WOULD I RATHER...

be in a band or have a solo career? ____________________

wear plaid shirts or suit jackets? ____________________

always wear a hat or always wear sunglasses? ____________________

live in Portland or Austin? ____________________

date a bandmate or my high school sweetheart? ____________________

play independent venues or arenas? ____________________

drive a vintage car or a motorcycle? ____________________

WHEN I'M AT
A PARTY, I ALWAYS
HOPE THEY'LL
PLAY THIS SONG:

______________________.

Location: ______________ Date: ______________

SONG TITLE: ______________

Artist ______________

Album: ______________

Label: ______________

Duration: ______________

Genre: ______________

Source: ______________

Who I want to share this song with: ______________

How I discovered this song: ______________

Playlists to put this song on: ______________

RATING:

Lyrics

Sound quality

Catchiness

Vocals

Mood it puts me in

Instrumentation

INSTRUMENTS IN THE SONG:

☐ ☐ ☐

☐ ☐ ☐

☐ ☐ ☐

☐ ☐ ☐

☐ Other: ______________

FAVORITE LYRIC:

THOUGHTS:

MOOD BOARD:

Location: ______ Date: ______

SONG TITLE: ______

Artist ______

Album: ______

Label: ______

Duration: ______

Genre: ______

Source: ______

Who I want to share this song with: ______

How I discovered this song: ______

Playlists to put this song on: ______

______

RATING:

Lyrics
Sound quality
Vocals
Instrumentation
Mood it puts me in
Catchiness

INSTRUMENTS IN THE SONG:

☐ ☐ ☐

☐ ☐ ☐

☐ ☐ ☐

☐ ☐ ☐

☐ Other: ______

______

FAVORITE LYRIC:

______

THOUGHTS:

MOOD BOARD:

Location: ______________ Date: ______________

SONG TITLE: ______________

Artist ______________

Album: ______________

Label: ______________

Duration: ______________

Genre: ______________

Source: ______________

Who I want to share this song with: ______________

How I discovered this song: ______________

Playlists to put this song on: ______________

____

RATING:

Lyrics

Sound quality

Catchiness

Vocals

Mood it puts me in

Instrumentation

INSTRUMENTS IN THE SONG:

☐ ☐ ☐

☐ ☐ ☐

☐ ☐ ☐

☐ ☐ ☐

☐ Other: ______________

____

FAVORITE LYRIC:

____

____

____

____

____

____

____

____

____

____

____

____

____

THOUGHTS:

MOOD BOARD:

A. PLAYLIST FOR

B. PLAYLIST FOR

TOP 25 SONGS OF ALL TIME

TITLE	ARTIST

GUILTY PLEASURE LIST

TITLE / ALBUM	ARTIST

Location: ____________ Date: ____________

SONG TITLE:

Artist

Album:

Label:

Duration:

Genre:

Source:

Who I want to share this song with:

How I discovered this song:

Playlists to put this song on:

RATING:

Lyrics

Sound quality

Catchiness

Vocals

Mood it puts me in

Instrumentation

INSTRUMENTS IN THE SONG:

☐ Other:

FAVORITE LYRIC:

THOUGHTS:

MOOD BOARD:

Location: ______________ Date: ______________

SONG TITLE:

Artist

Album:

Label:

Duration:

Genre:

Source:

Who I want to share this song with:

How I discovered this song:

Playlists to put this song on:

RATING:

Lyrics

Sound quality

Catchiness

Vocals

Mood it puts me in

Instrumentation

INSTRUMENTS IN THE SONG:

☐ Other:

FAVORITE LYRIC:

THOUGHTS:

MOOD BOARD:

Location: ____________ Date: ____________

SONG TITLE: ____________

Artist ____________

Album: ____________

Label: ____________

Duration: ____________

Genre: ____________

Source: ____________

Who I want to share this song with: ____________

How I discovered this song: ____________

Playlists to put this song on: ____________

RATING:

Lyrics

Sound quality

Catchiness

Vocals

Mood it puts me in

Instrumentation

INSTRUMENTS IN THE SONG:

☐ ☐ ☐

☐ ☐ ☐

☐ ☐ ☐

☐ ☐ ☐

☐ Other: ____________

FAVORITE LYRIC:

THOUGHTS:

MOOD BOARD:

ARTIST: ______________________________

ALBUM: ______________________________

FAVORITE SONG

LEAST FAVORITE SONG

I WAS ___ YEARS OLD WHEN I GOT MY FIRST ALBUM. I LISTENED TO THIS SONG OVER AND OVER AGAIN:

______________________.

GREAT LYRICS

Location: ______________ Date: ______________

SONG TITLE: ______________

Artist ______________

Album: ______________

Label: ______________

Duration: ______________

Genre: ______________

Source: ______________

Who I want to share this song with: ______________

How I discovered this song: ______________

Playlists to put this song on: ______________

____

RATING:

Lyrics

Sound quality

Vocals

Instrumentation

Mood it puts me in

Catchiness

INSTRUMENTS IN THE SONG:

☐ ☐ ☐

☐ ☐ ☐

☐ ☐ ☐

☐ ☐ ☐

☐ Other: ______________

____

FAVORITE LYRIC:

____

____

____

____

____

____

____

____

____

____

____

____

____

THOUGHTS:

MOOD BOARD:

Location: ______________ Date: ______________

SONG TITLE: ______________

Artist ______________

Album: ______________

Label: ______________

Duration: ______________

Genre: ______________

Source: ______________

Who I want to share this song with: ______________

How I discovered this song: ______________

Playlists to put this song on: ______________

____

RATING:

Lyrics

Sound quality

Catchiness

Vocals

Mood it puts me in

Instrumentation

INSTRUMENTS IN THE SONG:

☐ ☐ ☐

☐ ☐ ☐

☐ ☐ ☐

☐ ☐ ☐

☐ Other: ______________

____

FAVORITE LYRIC:

____

____

____

____

____

____

____

____

____

____

____

____

____

THOUGHTS:

MOOD BOARD:

Location: ______________ Date: ______________

SONG TITLE: ______________

Artist ______________

Album: ______________

Label: ______________

Duration: ______________

Genre: ______________

Source: ______________

Who I want to share this song with: ______________

How I discovered this song: ______________

Playlists to put this song on: ______________

____

RATING:

Lyrics

Sound quality

Vocals

Instrumentation

Mood it puts me in

Catchiness

INSTRUMENTS IN THE SONG:

☐ ☐ ☐

☐ ☐ ☐

☐ ☐ ☐

☐ ☐ ☐

☐ Other: ______________

____

FAVORITE LYRIC:

____

____

____

____

____

____

____

____

____

____

____

____

____

THOUGHTS:

MOOD BOARD:

IF I WERE...

A PUNK STAR

HOW WOULD I BE?

WOULD I RATHER...

be more like Joey Ramone or more like Patti Smith? ____________________

wear a leather jacket or leather pants? ____________________

get tattoos or piercings? ____________________

live in London or Berlin? ____________________

have a Mohawk or shave my head? ____________________

play in clubs or at house parties? ____________________

write songs against the government or songs against society? ____________________

WHEN I FEEL UPSET, I ALWAYS PLAY THIS SONG:

______________________________.

B. PLAYLIST FOR

SONGS I HATE

TITLE	ARTIST

GREAT SONGS TO SING ALONG TO

TITLE	ARTIST

Location: ______ Date: ______

SONG TITLE:

Artist ______

Album: ______

Label: ______

Duration: ______

Genre: ______

Source: ______

Who I want to share this song with: ______

How I discovered this song: ______

Playlists to put this song on: ______

RATING:

Lyrics

Sound quality

Catchiness

Vocals

Mood it puts me in

Instrumentation

INSTRUMENTS IN THE SONG:

☐ Other: ______

FAVORITE LYRIC:

THOUGHTS:

MOOD BOARD:

Location: ______ Date: ______

SONG TITLE:

Artist ______

Album: ______

Label: ______

Duration: ______

Genre: ______

Source: ______

Who I want to share this song with: ______

How I discovered this song: ______

Playlists to put this song on: ______

RATING:

Lyrics

Sound quality

Vocals

Instrumentation

Mood it puts me in

Catchiness

INSTRUMENTS IN THE SONG:

☐ ☐ ☐

☐ ☐ ☐

☐ ☐ ☐

☐ ☐ ☐

☐ Other: ______

FAVORITE LYRIC:

THOUGHTS:

MOOD BOARD:

Location: ____________ Date: ____________

SONG TITLE: ____________

Artist ____________

Album: ____________

Label: ____________

Duration: ____________

Genre: ____________

Source: ____________

Who I want to share this song with: ____________

How I discovered this song: ____________

Playlists to put this song on: ____________

RATING:

Lyrics
Sound quality
Catchiness
Vocals
Mood it puts me in
Instrumentation

INSTRUMENTS IN THE SONG:

☐ ☐ ☐

☐ ☐ ☐

☐ ☐ ☐

☐ ☐ ☐

☐ Other: ____________

FAVORITE LYRIC:

THOUGHTS:

MOOD BOARD:

ARTIST: ______________________

ALBUM: ______________________

FAVORITE SONG

LEAST FAVORITE SONG

I WAS ______ YEARS OLD WHEN I WENT TO MY FIRST CONCERT. THE VENUE WAS ______________. THE BAND WAS ______________. THE MOST AMAZING SONG OF THE NIGHT WAS ______________.

GREAT LYRICS

Location: ____________ Date: ____________

SONG TITLE:

Artist

Album:

Label:

Duration:

Genre:

Source:

Who I want to share this song with:

How I discovered this song:

Playlists to put this song on:

RATING:

Lyrics
Sound quality
Vocals
Instrumentation
Mood it puts me in
Catchiness

INSTRUMENTS IN THE SONG:

☐ ☐ ☐

☐ ☐ ☐

☐ ☐ ☐

☐ ☐ ☐

☐ Other:

FAVORITE LYRIC:

THOUGHTS:

MOOD BOARD:

Location: Date:

SONG TITLE:

Artist

Album:

Label:

Duration:

Genre:

Source:

Who I want to share this song with:

How I discovered this song:

Playlists to put this song on:

RATING:

Lyrics

Sound quality

Catchiness

Vocals

Mood it puts me in

Instrumentation

INSTRUMENTS IN THE SONG:

☐ ☐ ☐

☐ ☐ ☐

☐ ☐ ☐

☐ ☐ ☐

☐ Other:

FAVORITE LYRIC:

THOUGHTS:

MOOD BOARD:

Location: ______________ Date: ______________

SONG TITLE:

Artist

Album:

Label:

Duration:

Genre:

Source:

Who I want to share this song with:

How I discovered this song:

Playlists to put this song on:

RATING:

Lyrics

Sound quality

Catchiness

Vocals

Mood it puts me in

Instrumentation

INSTRUMENTS IN THE SONG:

- [ ]
- [ ]
- [ ]
- [ ]
- [ ]
- [ ]
- [ ]
- [ ]
- [ ]
- [ ]
- [ ]
- [ ]
- [ ] Other:

FAVORITE LYRIC:

THOUGHTS:

MOOD BOARD:

IF I WERE...

A HIP HOP STAR

HOW WOULD I BE?

WOULD I RATHER...

be a solo artist or be part of a group? ______________________________

be known for the speed of my raps or my songs' great hooks? ______________

win a Grammy for Best New Artist or have the song of the summer? __________

live in Chicago or New York? ____________________________________

be a Top 40 hip hop star or be big in the underground scene? _____________

be on a reality show or be famously private? __________________________

produce others' songs or be produced by a top producer? _________________

WHEN I'M DRIVING IN THE SUMMER-TIME, I ALWAYS PLAY THIS SONG:

____________________.

Location: ______________ Date: ______________

SONG TITLE: ______________

Artist ______________

Album: ______________

Label: ______________

Duration: ______________

Genre: ______________

Source: ______________

Who I want to share this song with: ______________

How I discovered this song: ______________

Playlists to put this song on: ______________

____

RATING:

Lyrics

Sound quality

Catchiness

Vocals

Mood it puts me in

Instrumentation

INSTRUMENTS IN THE SONG:

☐ ☐ ☐

☐ ☐ ☐

☐ ☐ ☐

☐ ☐ ☐

☐ Other: ______________

____

FAVORITE LYRIC:

____

____

____

____

____

____

____

____

____

____

____

____

____

THOUGHTS:

MOOD BOARD:

Location: ______ Date: ______

SONG TITLE: ______

Artist ______

Album: ______

Label: ______

Duration: ______

Genre: ______

Source: ______

Who I want to share this song with: ______

How I discovered this song: ______

Playlists to put this song on: ______

______

RATING:

Lyrics
Sound quality
Catchiness
Vocals
Mood it puts me in
Instrumentation

INSTRUMENTS IN THE SONG:

☐ ☐ ☐

☐ ☐ ☐

☐ ☐ ☐

☐ ☐ ☐

☐ Other: ______

______

FAVORITE LYRIC:

______

THOUGHTS:

MOOD BOARD:

Location: ____________ Date: ____________

SONG TITLE: ____________

Artist ____________

Album: ____________

Label: ____________

Duration: ____________

Genre: ____________

Source: ____________

Who I want to share this song with: ____________

How I discovered this song: ____________

Playlists to put this song on: ____________

____

RATING:

Lyrics
Sound quality
Vocals
Instrumentation
Mood it puts me in
Catchiness

INSTRUMENTS IN THE SONG:

☐ ☐ ☐

☐ ☐ ☐

☐ ☐ ☐

☐ ☐ ☐

☐ Other: ____________

____

FAVORITE LYRIC:

____

THOUGHTS:

MOOD BOARD:

A. PLAYLIST FOR

B. PLAYLIST FOR

BANDS I WANT TO SEE LIVE

ARTIST

BEST SHOWS I'VE BEEN TO

ARTIST	VENUE	DATE

Location: ____________ Date: ____________

SONG TITLE: ____________

Artist ____________

Album: ____________

Label: ____________

Duration: ____________

Genre: ____________

Source: ____________

Who I want to share this song with: ____________

How I discovered this song: ____________

Playlists to put this song on: ____________

RATING:

Lyrics

Sound quality

Vocals

Instrumentation

Mood it puts me in

Catchiness

INSTRUMENTS IN THE SONG:

☐ ☐ ☐

☐ ☐ ☐

☐ ☐ ☐

☐ ☐ ☐

☐ Other: ____________

FAVORITE LYRIC:

THOUGHTS:

MOOD BOARD:

Location: ______ Date: ______

SONG TITLE: ______

Artist ______

Album: ______

Label: ______

Duration: ______

Genre: ______

Source: ______

Who I want to share this song with: ______

How I discovered this song: ______

Playlists to put this song on: ______

______

RATING:

Lyrics
Sound quality
Vocals
Instrumentation
Mood it puts me in
Catchiness

INSTRUMENTS IN THE SONG:

☐ Other: ______

______

FAVORITE LYRIC:

______

THOUGHTS:

MOOD BOARD:

Location: ______ Date: ______

SONG TITLE: ______

Artist ______

Album: ______

Label: ______

Duration: ______

Genre: ______

Source: ______

Who I want to share this song with: ______

How I discovered this song: ______

Playlists to put this song on: ______

______

RATING:

Lyrics

Sound quality

Vocals

Instrumentation

Mood it puts me in

Catchiness

INSTRUMENTS IN THE SONG:

☐ ☐ ☐

☐ ☐ ☐

☐ ☐ ☐

☐ ☐ ☐

☐ Other: ______

______

FAVORITE LYRIC:

______

THOUGHTS:

MOOD BOARD:

ARTIST: ______________________________

ALBUM: ______________________________

FAVORITE SONG

LEAST FAVORITE SONG

THE FIRST BAND I EVER DISCOVERED ON MY OWN WAS ____________. THE FIRST PERSON I TOLD ABOUT THEM WAS ____________.

GREAT LYRICS

Location: ______________ Date: ______________

SONG TITLE: ______________

Artist ______________

Album: ______________

Label: ______________

Duration: ______________

Genre: ______________

Source: ______________

Who I want to share this song with: ______________

How I discovered this song: ______________

Playlists to put this song on: ______________

____

RATING:

Lyrics

Sound quality

Catchiness

Vocals

Mood it puts me in

Instrumentation

INSTRUMENTS IN THE SONG:

☐ ☐ ☐

☐ ☐ ☐

☐ ☐ ☐

☐ ☐ ☐

☐ Other: ______________

____

FAVORITE LYRIC:

____

____

____

____

____

____

____

____

____

____

____

____

____

THOUGHTS:

MOOD BOARD:

Location: ______ Date: ______

SONG TITLE: ______

Artist ______

Album: ______

Label: ______

Duration: ______

Genre: ______

Source: ______

Who I want to share this song with: ______

How I discovered this song: ______

Playlists to put this song on: ______

______

RATING:

Lyrics

Sound quality

Vocals

Instrumentation

Mood it puts me in

Catchiness

INSTRUMENTS IN THE SONG:

☐ Other: ______

______

FAVORITE LYRIC:

______

THOUGHTS:

MOOD BOARD:

Location: ______________________ Date: ______________

SONG TITLE: ______________________

Artist ______________________

Album: ______________________

Label: ______________________

Duration: ______________________

Genre: ______________________

Source: ______________________

Who I want to share this song with: ______________________

How I discovered this song: ______________________

Playlists to put this song on: ______________________

____

RATING:

Lyrics

Sound quality

Vocals

Instrumentation

Mood it puts me in

Catchiness

INSTRUMENTS IN THE SONG:

- [ ] Other: ______________________

____

FAVORITE LYRIC:

____

THOUGHTS:

MOOD BOARD:

IF I WERE...

A JAZZ STAR

HOW WOULD I BE?

WOULD I RATHER...

take lots of solos or play it cool? ______________________________

make music people can swing to or music people call brilliant? ______________

scat or croon? ______________________________

live in New Orleans or Pittsburgh? ______________________________

have an instrumental band or one with vocals? ______________________

play Preservation Hall or Carnegie Hall? ______________________

play multiple instruments very well or play only one instrument like a prodigy?

____

I THINK THE NATIONAL ANTHEM SHOULD BE THIS SONG:

________.

Location: ______________________ Date: ____________________

SONG TITLE: ______________________

Artist ______________________

Album: ______________________

Label: ______________________

Duration: ______________________

Genre: ______________________

Source: ______________________

Who I want to share this song with: ______________________

How I discovered this song: ______________________

Playlists to put this song on: ______________________

____

RATING:

Lyrics

Sound quality

Vocals

Instrumentation

Mood it puts me in

Catchiness

INSTRUMENTS IN THE SONG:

☐ ☐ ☐

☐ ☐ ☐

☐ ☐ ☐

☐ ☐ ☐

☐ Other: ______________________

____

FAVORITE LYRIC:

____

____

____

____

____

____

____

____

____

____

____

____

____

THOUGHTS:

MOOD BOARD:

Location: ______ Date: ______

SONG TITLE: ______

Artist ______

Album: ______

Label: ______

Duration: ______

Genre: ______

Source: ______

Who I want to share this song with: ______

How I discovered this song: ______

Playlists to put this song on: ______

RATING:

Lyrics

Sound quality

Vocals

Instrumentation

Mood it puts me in

Catchiness

INSTRUMENTS IN THE SONG:

☐ Other: ______

FAVORITE LYRIC:

THOUGHTS:

MOOD BOARD:

Location: ______________________ Date: ______________________

SONG TITLE: ______________________

Artist ______________________

Album: ______________________

Label: ______________________

Duration: ______________________

Genre: ______________________

Source: ______________________

Who I want to share this song with: ______________________

How I discovered this song: ______________________

Playlists to put this song on: ______________________

____

RATING:

Lyrics

Sound quality

Vocals

Instrumentation

Mood it puts me in

Catchiness

INSTRUMENTS IN THE SONG:

☐ ☐ ☐

☐ ☐ ☐

☐ ☐ ☐

☐ ☐ ☐

☐ Other: ______________________

____

FAVORITE LYRIC:

____

THOUGHTS:

MOOD BOARD:

A. PLAYLIST FOR

B. PLAYLIST FOR

NEW BANDS TO CHECK OUT

ARTIST

TITLE / ALBUM	ARTIST

Location: ______ Date: ______

SONG TITLE:

Artist

Album:

Label:

Duration:

Genre:

Source:

Who I want to share this song with:

How I discovered this song:

Playlists to put this song on:

RATING:

Lyrics

Sound quality

Vocals

Instrumentation

Mood it puts me in

Catchiness

INSTRUMENTS IN THE SONG:

☐ Other:

FAVORITE LYRIC:

THOUGHTS:

MOOD BOARD:

Location: ______________ Date: ______________

SONG TITLE: ______________

Artist ______________

Album: ______________

Label: ______________

Duration: ______________

Genre: ______________

Source: ______________

Who I want to share this song with: ______________

How I discovered this song: ______________

Playlists to put this song on: ______________

RATING:

Lyrics

Sound quality

Vocals

Instrumentation

Mood it puts me in

Catchiness

INSTRUMENTS IN THE SONG:

☐ Other: ______________

FAVORITE LYRIC:

THOUGHTS:

MOOD BOARD:

Location: ______ Date: ______

SONG TITLE: ______

Artist ______

Album: ______

Label: ______

Duration: ______

Genre: ______

Source: ______

Who I want to share this song with: ______

How I discovered this song: ______

Playlists to put this song on: ______

______

RATING:

Lyrics

Sound quality

Catchiness

Vocals

Mood it puts me in

Instrumentation

INSTRUMENTS IN THE SONG:

☐ ☐ ☐

☐ ☐ ☐

☐ ☐ ☐

☐ ☐ ☐

☐ Other: ______

______

FAVORITE LYRIC:

______

THOUGHTS:

MOOD BOARD:

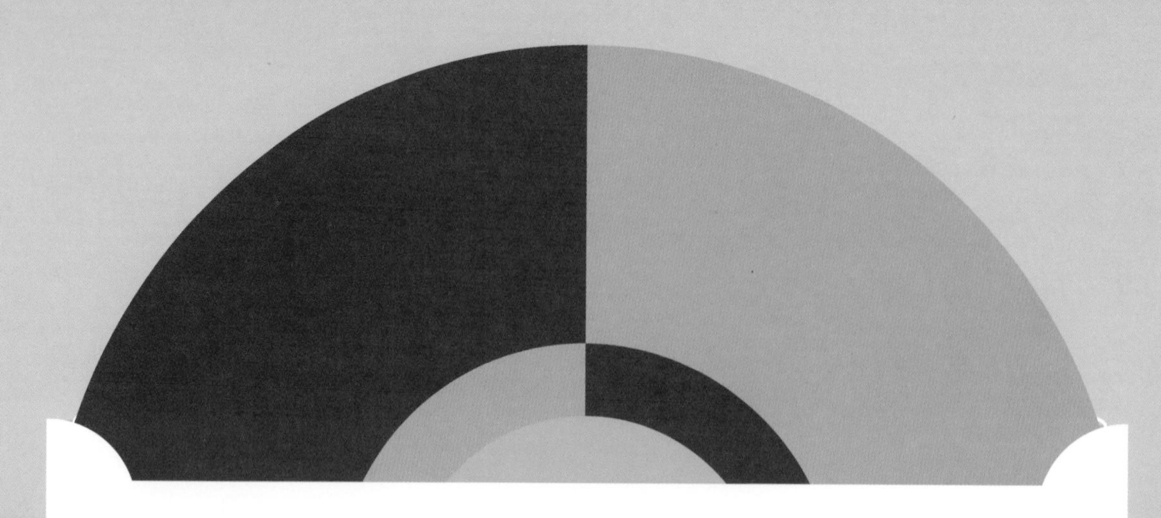

ARTIST: ______________________

ALBUM: ______________________

FAVORITE SONG

LEAST FAVORITE SONG

THE FIRST SONG I LEARNED ALL THE WORDS TO WAS

_______________.

THE FIRST SONG I DID KARAOKE TO WAS _______________.

GREAT LYRICS

Location: ______________ Date: ______________

SONG TITLE: ______________

Artist ______________

Album: ______________

Label: ______________

Duration: ______________

Genre: ______________

Source: ______________

Who I want to share this song with: ______________

How I discovered this song: ______________

Playlists to put this song on: ______________

____

RATING:

Lyrics

Sound quality

Vocals

Instrumentation

Mood it puts me in

Catchiness

INSTRUMENTS IN THE SONG:

☐ ☐ ☐

☐ ☐ ☐

☐ ☐ ☐

☐ ☐ ☐

☐ Other: ______________

____

FAVORITE LYRIC:

____

____

____

____

____

____

____

____

____

____

____

____

____

THOUGHTS:

MOOD BOARD:

Location: ____________ Date: ____________

SONG TITLE: ____________

Artist ____________

Album: ____________

Label: ____________

Duration: ____________

Genre: ____________

Source: ____________

Who I want to share this song with: ____________

How I discovered this song: ____________

Playlists to put this song on: ____________

____

RATING:

Lyrics

Sound quality

Catchiness

Vocals

Mood it puts me in

Instrumentation

INSTRUMENTS IN THE SONG:

☐ Other: ____________

____

FAVORITE LYRIC:

____

THOUGHTS:

MOOD BOARD:

Location: ______ Date: ______

SONG TITLE: ______

Artist ______

Album: ______

Label: ______

Duration: ______

Genre: ______

Source: ______

Who I want to share this song with: ______

How I discovered this song: ______

Playlists to put this song on: ______

RATING:

Lyrics
Sound quality
Vocals
Instrumentation
Mood it puts me in
Catchiness

INSTRUMENTS IN THE SONG:

Other: ______

FAVORITE LYRIC:

THOUGHTS:

MOOD BOARD:

IF I WERE...

A COUNTRY STAR

HOW WOULD I BE?

WOULD I RATHER...

be an outlaw rebel or an alt-country rocker? ______________________

play only acoustic sets or write only narrative songs? ______________________

record at Muscle Shoals or Third Man Records? ______________________

live in Nashville or Austin? ______________________

have a gravelly, distinctive voice or perfect pitch? ______________________

write songs for someone else or sing songs someone else writes? ______________________

always wear a bolo tie or always wear cowboy boots? ______________________

IF I COULD HEAR ONLY ONE SONG FOR THE REST OF MY LIFE, IT WOULD BE:

________________________.

Location: ____________ Date: ____________

SONG TITLE: ____________

Artist ____________

Album: ____________

Label: ____________

Duration: ____________

Genre: ____________

Source: ____________

Who I want to share this song with: ____________

How I discovered this song: ____________

Playlists to put this song on: ____________

RATING:

Lyrics
Sound quality
Vocals
Instrumentation
Mood it puts me in
Catchiness

INSTRUMENTS IN THE SONG:

☐ ☐ ☐
☐ ☐ ☐
☐ ☐ ☐
☐ ☐ ☐

☐ Other: ____________

FAVORITE LYRIC:

THOUGHTS:

MOOD BOARD:

Location: ____________ Date: ____________

SONG TITLE: ____________

Artist ____________

Album: ____________

Label: ____________

Duration: ____________

Genre: ____________

Source: ____________

Who I want to share this song with: ____________

How I discovered this song: ____________

Playlists to put this song on: ____________

RATING:

Lyrics

Sound quality

Vocals

Instrumentation

Mood it puts me in

Catchiness

INSTRUMENTS IN THE SONG:

☐ Other: ____________

FAVORITE LYRIC:

THOUGHTS:

MOOD BOARD:

Location: ______________ Date: ______________

SONG TITLE: ______________

Artist ______________

Album: ______________

Label: ______________

Duration: ______________

Genre: ______________

Source: ______________

Who I want to share this song with: ______________

How I discovered this song: ______________

Playlists to put this song on: ______________

____

RATING:

Lyrics

Sound quality

Catchiness

Vocals

Mood it puts me in

Instrumentation

INSTRUMENTS IN THE SONG:

☐ ☐ ☐

☐ ☐ ☐

☐ ☐ ☐

☐ ☐ ☐

☐ Other: ______________

____

FAVORITE LYRIC:

____

____

____

____

____

____

____

____

____

____

____

____

____

THOUGHTS:

MOOD BOARD:

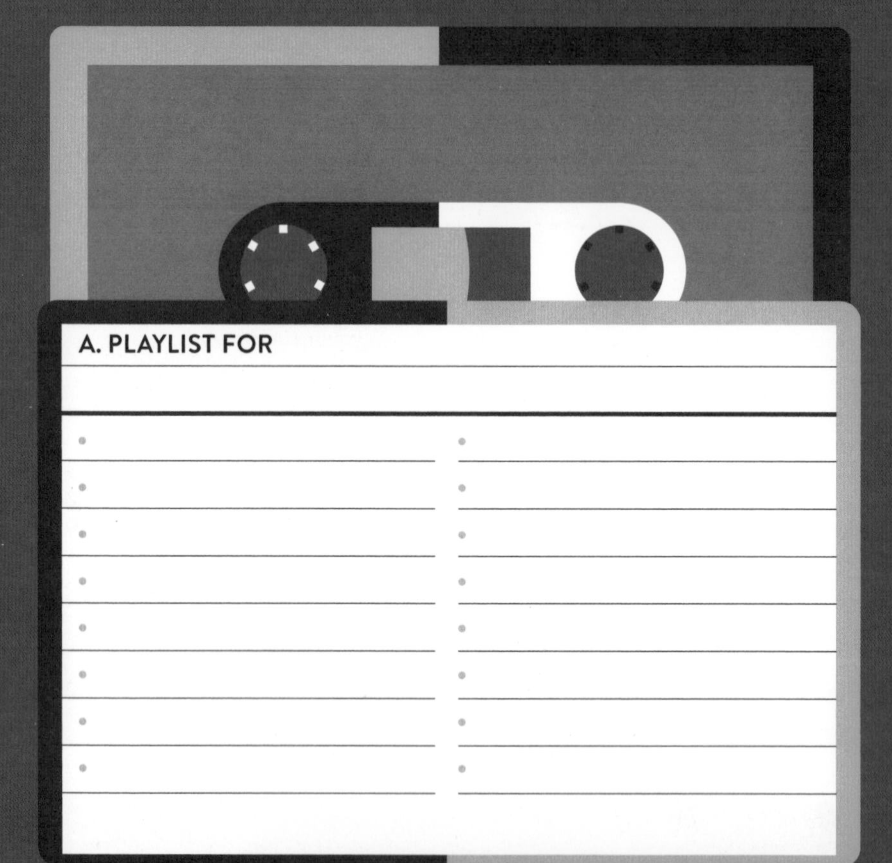
A. PLAYLIST FOR

B. PLAYLIST FOR

TOP 25 BANDS OF ALL TIME

ARTIST

BEST SONGS TO DANCE TO

TITLE	ARTIST

Location: ______________ Date: ______________

SONG TITLE: ______________

Artist ______________

Album: ______________

Label: ______________

Duration: ______________

Genre: ______________

Source: ______________

Who I want to share this song with: ______________

How I discovered this song: ______________

Playlists to put this song on: ______________

____

RATING:

Lyrics

Sound quality

Vocals

Instrumentation

Mood it puts me in

Catchiness

INSTRUMENTS IN THE SONG:

☐ ☐ ☐

☐ ☐ ☐

☐ ☐ ☐

☐ ☐ ☐

☐ Other: ______________

____

FAVORITE LYRIC:

____

____

____

____

____

____

____

____

____

____

____

____

____

THOUGHTS:

MOOD BOARD:

Location: ______________ Date: ______________

SONG TITLE: ______________

Artist ______________

Album: ______________

Label: ______________

Duration: ______________

Genre: ______________

Source: ______________

Who I want to share this song with: ______________

How I discovered this song: ______________

Playlists to put this song on: ______________

____

RATING:

Lyrics

Sound quality

Vocals

Instrumentation

Mood it puts me in

Catchiness

INSTRUMENTS IN THE SONG:

☐ ☐ ☐

☐ ☐ ☐

☐ ☐ ☐

☐ ☐ ☐

☐ Other: ______________

____

FAVORITE LYRIC:

____

____

____

____

____

____

____

____

____

____

____

____

____

THOUGHTS:

MOOD BOARD:

Location: ______ Date: ______

SONG TITLE: ______

Artist ______

Album: ______

Label: ______

Duration: ______

Genre: ______

Source: ______

Who I want to share this song with: ______

How I discovered this song: ______

Playlists to put this song on: ______

RATING:

Lyrics

Sound quality

Vocals

Instrumentation

Mood it puts me in

Catchiness

INSTRUMENTS IN THE SONG:

☐ ☐ ☐

☐ ☐ ☐

☐ ☐ ☐

☐ ☐ ☐

☐ Other: ______

FAVORITE LYRIC:

THOUGHTS:

MOOD BOARD:

ARTIST: ______________________________

ALBUM: ______________________________

FAVORITE SONG

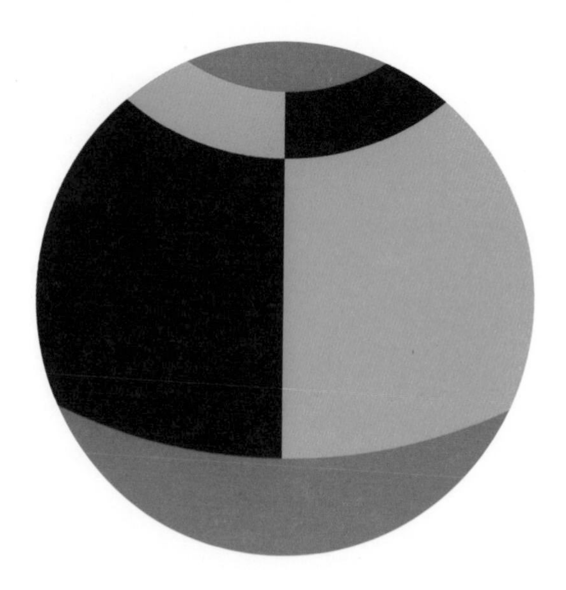

LEAST FAVORITE SONG

I WAS ___ YEARS OLD WHEN I FIRST REALIZED THAT A SONG COULD CHANGE MY BAD MOOD ENTIRELY. A SONG THAT ALWAYS DOES IS: ________.

GREAT LYRICS

Close your eyes. Pick one word from the left page, and another one from the right page.

MISCELLANEOUS	ADJECTIVE	ADJECTIVE	PREPOSITION
THE	ODD	ROTTEN	UNDER
MY	TARADIDDLE	SUPERSONIC	BEHIND
YOUR	WICKED	GENIUS	ON TOP
HIS	MADCAP	MOUTHY	BESIDE
HER	SAVVY	TWISTED	AMONG
A / AN	SWEET	DINGY	INSIDE
[PICK A NUMBER!]	ARCADIAN	HAIRLESS	OUTSIDE
BE	ZEALOUS	POMPOUS	BEYOND
FOR	GREEN	JAGGED	BELOW
THIS	[PICK A NUMBER!]	SWEET	UNDERNEATH
THAT	THIN	SERENE	ACROSS
NOT	YOUNG	SASSY	EXCEPT
ANOTHER	JOYFUL	GLITTERY	DURING
NEXT	BIG	GOLDEN	OPPOSITE
BUT	BEST	BUFF	WITHIN